# SCIENCEWORKS!

# Join a Shark Expedition

By Suzy Gazlay

Shark Consultant: Salvador Jorgensen

Series Consultant: Kirk A. Janowiak

**Gareth Stevens**
Publishing

Please visit our web site at www.garethstevens.com. For a free catalog describing our list of high-quality books, call 1-800-542-2595 (USA) or 1-800-387-3178 (Canada). Our fax: 1-877-542-2596

Library of Congress Cataloging-in-Publication Data available upon request from publisher.
ISBN-13: 978-0-8368-8932-1 (lib. bdg.)
ISBN-10: 0-8368-8932-0 (lib. bdg.)
ISBN-13: 978-0-8368-8939-0 (softcover)
ISBN-10: 0-8368-8939-8 (softcover)

This North American edition first published in 2008 by
**Gareth Stevens Publishing**
A Weekly Reader® Company
1 Reader's Digest Road
Pleasantville, NY 10570-7000 USA

This U.S. edition copyright © 2008 by Gareth Stevens, Inc. Original edition copyright © 2007 by ticktock Media Ltd.
First published in Great Britain in 2007 by ticktock Media Ltd., Unit 2, Orchard Business Centre, North Farm Road,
Tunbridge Wells, Kent, TN2 3XF United Kingdom

ticktock Project Editor: Jo Hanks
ticktock Designer: Graham Rich
With thanks to: Sara Greasley and Anna Brett

Gareth Stevens Editor: Jayne Keedle
Gareth Stevens Creative Director: Lisa Donovan
Gareth Stevens Graphic Designer: Ken Crossland

Printed in the United States of America

1 2 3 4 5 6 7 8 9 10 09 08 07

## SUZY GAZLAY

Suzy Gazlay (M.A. Integrated Math/Science Education) is a teacher and writer who has worked with students of all ages. She has also served as a science specialist, curriculum developer, and consultant in varying capacities. She is the recipient of a Presidential Award for Excellence in Math and Science Teaching. Now retired from full-time classroom teaching, she continues to write, consult, and work with educators and children, particularly in science and music education. Her many interests include music, environmental issues, marine biology, and the outdoors.

## KIRK A. JANOWIAK

Kirk A. Janowiak (B.S. Biology & Natural Resources, M.S. Ecology & Animal Behavior, M.S. Science Education) has enjoyed teaching students from pre-school through college. He has been awarded the National Association of Biology Teachers' Outstanding Biology Teacher Award and was honored to be a finalist for the Presidential Award for Excellence in Math & Science Teaching. Kirk currently teaches Biology and Environmental Science and enjoys a wide range of interests from music to the art of roasting coffee.

## SALVADOR JORGENSEN

Salvador Jorgensen (Ph.D.) is a postdoctoral scholar working at Stanford University's Hopkins Marine Station and the Monterey Bay Aquarium in California. He is researching the movement and population structure of white sharks in the eastern Pacific Ocean using tagging and genetics. During graduate school Dr. Jorgensen performed his field studies as a Fulbright scholar in Mexico's Gulf of California (Sea of Cortez) studying the movements of tunas and scalloped hammerhead sharks around seamounts.

# CONTENTS

This book will help students develop these vital science skills:

- Asking questions about objects, organisms, and events in the environment
- Using data to construct a reasonable explanation
- Communicating investigations and explanations
- Understanding properties of objects and materials
- Identifying position and motion of objects
- Identifying a simple problem
- Proposing a solution
- Implementing proposed solutions
- Evaluating a problem or design
- Communicating a problem, design, and solution
- Understanding science and technology
- Distinguishing between natural objects and objects made by humans
- Understanding the characteristics of organisms
- Understanding life cycles of organisms
- Identifying organisms and their environment

**Supports the National Science Education Standards (NSES) for Grades K–4**

# HOW TO USE THIS BOOK

**S**cience is important in the lives of people everywhere. We use science at home and at school. In fact, we use science all the time. You need to know science to understand how the world works. A shark biologist needs to understand science in order to gather information about sharks' behavior. He or she uses this information to educate people and to try to protect sharks. With this book, you'll use science to research and track sharks.

This exciting science book is very easy to use. Check out what's inside!

## INTRODUCTION

Do you have what it takes to be a shark biologist? Find out as you track and research sharks.

## FACTFILE

Read easy-to-understand information about how shark biology works.

### STAYING WARM IN COLD WATER

**T**he Sun is rising as you and your crew head out to sea. You are going to an elephant seal colony on a faraway beach on the California coast. Great white sharks will be offshore, waiting for a chance to catch their next meal. Elephant seals aren't easy prey. These huge beasts have lots of blubber. They can weigh more than 5,000 pounds (2,270 kilograms)! If the shark doesn't strike just right, an elephant seal can put up a tough fight. You've seen great white sharks with the scars to prove it!

### 🦈 FACTFILE

- If you were cold-blooded, like most fish, your body temperature would be a chilly 40° Fahrenheit (4° Celsius).
- Great white sharks are warm-bodied. They can keep some parts of their body warmer than the surrounding water. That helps them swim fast and survive in cold water, where seals live.
- Eating, swimming, and other physical activities generate heat. Most fish lose that heat from the surface of their bodies. The great white shark's powerful muscles are near the center of its body. That is where most of the blood is, far away from the skin, where heat can be lost.

16

4

# WORKSTATION

Learn how marine biologists interpret shark data from diagrams, charts, graphs, and maps.

# CHALLENGE QUESTIONS

Now that you understand the science, put it into practice.

## WORKSTATION

**You've been gathering data about the types of prey eaten by great white sharks along this coast.**

Great white sharks have to be picky eaters because they need high-fat food for fuel. They may eat other prey, but animals with lots of blubber are their food of choice. Seals are a shark's ideal dinner. As your boat approaches the seal colony, you see a great white shark attack a young elephant seal. You count the number of animals you've seen great white sharks eat. Below is your list so far.

**Elephant seal** 25

**California sea lion** 15

**Dead whale carcass** 6

**Northern fur seal** 10

**Pelican** 2

**Jellyfish** 1

**Sea turtle** 3

**Seagull** 1

**Other sharks** 5

**Tuna** 6

**Halibut** 4

**Mackerel** 8

**Harbor seal** 15

**Salmon** 6

**Porpoise** 1

## Q CHALLENGE QUESTIONS

1. Which four kinds of prey were attacked most often?
2. What do those four animals have in common?
3. Why would seals be a particularly good choice of food?
4. Why would a blubbery dead whale be a good choice of food for a great white shark?

17

# IF YOU NEED HELP!

## TIPS FOR SCIENCE SUCCESS

On page 30, you will find tips to help you with your science work.

## ANSWERS

Turn to page 31 to check your answers. (*Try all the activities and questions before you take a look at the answers.*)

## GLOSSARY

Turn to page 32 for definitions of important science words.

# SHARK BIOLOGIST

**S**ome people fear sharks—but you don't! You are a shark biologist. Your laboratory is in Monterey, California, next to a large bay that opens into the Pacific Ocean. You are an expert on great white sharks and hammerhead sharks. You study how they live. You want to know how far they travel and where they go. You learn about sharks by visiting the places where they gather. You help protect sharks. The local aquarium asks you to come talk to visitors about your work.

## FACTFILE

- There are more than 460 known species, or types, of sharks.
- Some sharks lay eggs that hatch in the water. In other species, babies are born live and are able to swim.
- Most sharks live in salt water, but some live in freshwater.
- Sharks can be found in both shallow and very deep waters.
- Some sharks stick close to home. Others travel long distances.
- Sharks cannot swim backward. Most must swim forward in order to breathe.
- Sharks do not normally attack people.

A school of gray reef sharks looks for food.

You show your audience photographs of different types of sharks from all over the world. They are amazed by the diversity, or variety of species.

| Name | Whale shark | Great white shark | Oceanic whitetip shark |
|---|---|---|---|
| Length | Up to 46 feet (14 m) | Up to 23 feet (7 m) | Up to 13 feet (4 m) |
| Diet | Plankton, small fish | Fish, marine mammals | Fish, turtles, birds, garbage |

| Name | Sawfish shark | Spined pygmy shark | Frilled shark |
|---|---|---|---|
| Length | Up to 25 feet (7.6 m) | 7–8 inches (20 cm) | Up to 6 feet (1.8 m) |
| Diet | Fish, shellfish, squid | Squid, shrimp, fish | Squid, fish |

 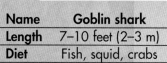 

| Name | Goblin shark | Scalloped hammerhead shark | Wobbegong shark |
|---|---|---|---|
| Length | 7–10 feet (2–3 m) | Up to 14 feet (4.3 m) | 9–10 feet (3 m) |
| Diet | Fish, squid, crabs | Fish, rays, squid, shellfish | Fish, shellfish, octopus |

 CHALLENGE QUESTIONS

You study the chart above to answer the following questions:

1. Which of these sharks is the largest?
2. Which of these sharks is the smallest?
3. How many of these sharks grow to 10 feet or longer?
4. Name three foods eaten by most of these sharks.

**A**s a shark expert, you're often asked to provide information to the public. Today, you're designing a display for a local aquarium. You want to show how a shark's body works. Sharks can look very different from one another. Even so, their bodies are designed in similar ways to help them survive.

A **pectoral fin** on each side helps with swimming, balance, and turning.

A pair of **pelvic fins** helps with balance and mating.

## FACTFILE

### All sharks have a similar skeleton.

- The skeleton is not made of bone. Instead, it is made of strong, flexible cartilage. That's the same material that gives shape to your ears.

- Cartilage bends easily, which helps sharks make tight turns. It is lighter than bone and helps keep the shark from sinking.

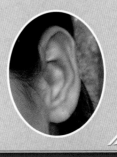

The hammerhead shark has some very strange features! Even so, it has the same structure as other sharks.

One or more **dorsal fins** are used for balance and steering.

The strong **caudal fin**, or tail, pushes the shark through the water.

The **anal fin** is used for balance.

**These are some interesting shark features.**

### SHARK SKIN

- A shark's skin is covered with toothlike scales called denticles. This picture shows what denticles look like under a microscope.

- Most denticles point backward. If you rub the shark's skin from front to back, the denticles feel smooth. If you rub the shark the other way, the denticles are rough enough to hurt you.

- The denticles' shape helps the shark swim more smoothly and quietly through the water.

### SHARK SNOUT

- The shark uses its nostrils for smelling, not breathing.

- A sharp sense of smell helps a shark find food.

### SHARK TEETH

- Some sharks have up to 3,000 teeth at any one time.

- The teeth are arranged in rows, usually about five rows at a time.

- If a tooth is worn down, damaged, or lost, a tooth in the next row replaces it.

## (Q) CHALLENGE QUESTIONS

Aquarium visitors ask you these questions:

1. What happens when a shark loses or damages a tooth?

2. Why does a shark's skin feel rough?

3. What are the five different types of fins?

4. Which two types of fins have the most to do with changing direction?

# SHARK KILLERS

**S**ome beachgoers found a dead shark washed up on the shore. You take the body back to your lab. You decide to do a medical examination of the dead animal. That should help you find out why the shark died. Was it sick? Did it eat something that made it sick? Did it stop eating? Was it injured? Did it have a disease? To find out, you need to look inside the shark.

 **FACTFILE**

**Sharks breathe through their gills:**

- There are several pairs of gill slits on either side of the shark's head.
- Water passes in through the mouth and over the gills. Blood vessels inside fleshy gill filaments take in oxygen from water.
- In order to breathe, many sharks must either be swimming forward or facing into a current. Some move their gill covers or use their fins to pump water across their gills.

In this cross section of a shark, you can see how its gills look from the inside.

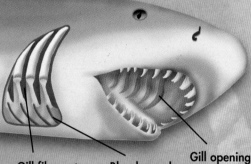

Gill filaments take in oxygen from the water.

Blood vessels pass oxygen around the body.

Gill opening

## You put the shark on the lab table and get to work:

**First you look for signs of injury.**

• You don't see cuts or bruises that might have come from fighting. You also don't see any injuries to suggest it was hit by a boat.

**You carefully cut into the shark's belly. You examine the liver. It looks normal.**

• The liver stores extra fats as oil. The oil is lighter than water. It helps the shark float.

**Next you look at the shark's gills. Under a microscope, you see what killed this shark.**

• The shark's gills are full of parasites. A parasite is a tiny creature that lives on another animal, often harming it. Tiny, shrimp-like parasites called copepods feed on sharks' skin and blood. Copepods fed on blood from this shark's gills. That means the shark received less oxygen, which made it weak.

The liver of this dead basking shark is circled in red. The liver is a shark's largest organ. It can be as much as 25 percent of the shark's total weight.

A marine copepod

## CHALLENGE QUESTIONS

You fill out a report that lists what you found:

1. What caused the shark to die?

2. The largest organ in the shark's body looked normal. What organ is that?

3. How do you know the shark wasn't attacked by another shark?

4. What four things can a shark do to keep water flowing across its gills?

This great white shark died when it was caught in a fishing net. Its injuries were caused by struggling against the net.

# LEAPING SHARKS!

You've worked with sharks for a long time, but you're still amazed at the things they can do. This is one of those moments. As you and your team watch in awe, a great white shark suddenly breaks through the surface of the water. Its long body arches through the air. Then it's gone in a flash. As the shark dives back into the water, it showers you with spray. When a shark leaps out of the water like that, it's called breaching. You want to find out why the shark breaches.

 **FACTFILE**

Despite its large size and weight, the body of a great white shark is well designed to breach.

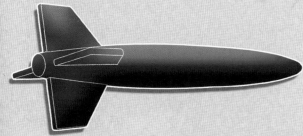

- A shark's body is shaped like a torpedo (above). This shape helps the shark to move quickly through the water.

- The strong ridge at the base of the tail works with powerful muscles in the middle of the body. Together, they propel the shark out of the water.

## WORKSTATION

### Why does a great white shark breach?

To answer that question, you need to make some observations. Here are two possible explanations and clues that might help explain why sharks breach:

- If sharks breach while feeding, you would expect to see prey nearby. Prey are animals hunted for food.
- If breaching has to do with mating behavior, you would expect to see possible mates nearby.

You observe eight different great white sharks breaching. You name each shark you see with a different letter. Your notes look like this:

| Breaching sharks | Male or female? | Other sharks observed? | Prey observed? |
|---|---|---|---|
| A | Male | None | None |
| B | Female | 1 female | 1 seal |
| C | Female | 2 males | 1 sea lion |
| D | Male | 2 males | 1 seal |
| E | Female | None | 1 sea lion |
| F | Male | None | 1 seal, 1 tuna |
| G | Female | 1 female, 1 male | None |
| H | Male | 1 male | 1 seal |

**Q** CHALLENGE QUESTIONS

1. How many times was a shark of the opposite sex seen near the area where a shark was breaching?

2. How many times were seals or sea lions present?

3. Do you think it is more likely that sharks breach because of feeding or mating behavior?

4. Why did you reach this conclusion?

# TOP PREDATORS

**A**s predators, sharks play an important role in keeping marine life balanced. You've heard that there aren't many hammerhead sharks left in the Sea of Cortez in Mexico. They were once the sea's top predators. Many of them have been hunted and killed. What will happen to the marine life in the area if they are gone? You decide to investigate.

 **FACTFILE**

All living things are part of a food chain. Plants are called producers because they make their own food. Animals are consumers. They get the food they need by eating producers and other consumers. This chart shows who eats what.

**Secondary carnivores** are meat eaters that eat other carnivores. They are usually the top predators. No other animal eats them.

↑

**Primary carnivores** are meat eaters that eat both omnivores and herbivores.

↑              ↑

**1.** **Herbivores** eat only plants.    **2.** **Omnivores** eat both plants and animals.

↑

**Producers**, such as plants, make their own food.

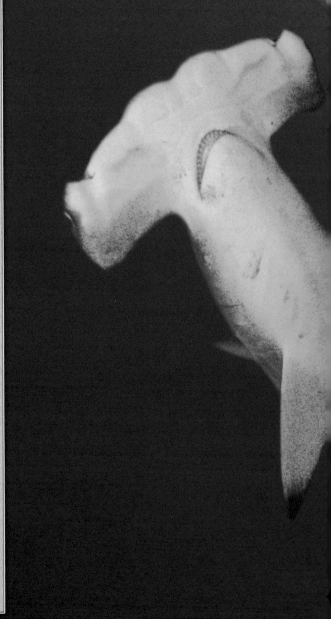

## WORKSTATION

### Sea of Cortez Food Chain Investigation

Both primary and secondary carnivores are predators. If a predator is removed from a food chain, the population of animals that it used to eat will increase. Then there will be more of those animals to eat the animals below them on the food chain.

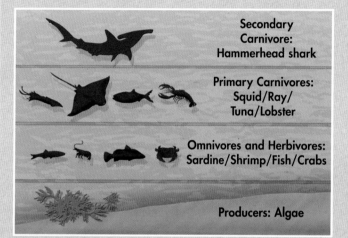

Secondary Carnivore: Hammerhead shark

Primary Carnivores: Squid/Ray/Tuna/Lobster

Omnivores and Herbivores: Sardine/Shrimp/Fish/Crabs

Producers: Algae

To find out who eats what, you look inside the stomachs of three of the predators. Here's what you find:

| Sardine | Hammerhead shark | Squid |
|---------|------------------|-------|
| Tiny crabs | Ray | Crabs |
| Shrimp | Tuna | Shrimp |
| Algae | Squid | Sardine |
| Fish eggs | Lobster | Fish |

## Q CHALLENGE QUESTIONS

1. Put sardines, hammerhead sharks, and squid in order in a food chain, from highest to lowest level.

2. If hammerheads are gone from the Sea of Cortez, which populations of animals will probably increase?

3. If the squid population increases, which animals will be eaten in even greater numbers?

4. What could happen to the sardine population if the sharks are gone? Why?

The Sun is rising as you and your crew head out to sea. You are going to an elephant seal colony on a faraway beach on the California coast. Great white sharks will be offshore, waiting for a chance to catch their next meal. Elephant seals aren't easy prey. These huge beasts have lots of blubber. They can weigh more than 5,000 pounds (2,270 kilograms)! If the shark doesn't strike just right, an elephant seal can put up a tough fight. You've seen great white sharks with the scars to prove it!

## FACTFILE

- If you were cold-blooded, like most fish, your body temperature would be a chilly 40° Fahrenheit (4° Celsius).
- Great white sharks are warm-bodied. They can keep some parts of their body warmer than the surrounding water. That helps them swim fast and survive in cold water, where seals live.
- Eating, swimming, and other physical activities generate heat. Most fish lose that heat from the surface of their bodies. The great white shark's powerful muscles are near the center of its body. That is where most of the blood is, far away from the skin, where heat can be lost.

## You've been gathering data about the types of prey eaten by great white sharks along this coast.

Great white sharks have to be picky eaters because they need high-fat food for fuel. They may eat other prey, but animals with lots of blubber are their food of choice. Seals are a shark's ideal dinner. As your boat approaches the seal colony, you see a great white shark attack a young elephant seal. You count the number of animals you've seen great white sharks eat. Below is your list so far.

**Elephant seal** 25

**California sea lion** 15

**Dead whale carcass** 6

**Northern fur seal** 10

**Pelican** 2

**Jellyfish** 1

**Sea turtle** 3

**Seagull** 1

**Other sharks** 5

**Tuna** 6

**Halibut** 4

**Mackerel** 8

**Harbor seal** 15

**Salmon** 6

**Porpoise** 1

## Q CHALLENGE QUESTIONS

1. Which four kinds of prey were attacked most often?
2. What do those four animals have in common?
3. Why would seals be a particularly good choice of food?
4. Why would a blubbery dead whale be a good choice of food for a great white shark?

17

# HIT OR MISS?

Your phone rings. The caller is a reporter who wants information about great white sharks. A surfer has been attacked near a beach in Southern California. Thankfully, the surfer was not injured—just badly frightened. His surfboard, however, is a different story. The shark took a huge bite out of it, leaving jagged teeth marks. The reporter thinks, as many people do, that sharks have poor eyesight. Otherwise, why would this one have bitten the board instead of the surfer? You explain what really happened.

##  FACTFILE

You tell the reporter that shark attacks are rare. Other animals injure or kill many more people than sharks do. You have the data to back up your statement.

| Animal | Approximate number of people killed by animals in the United States from 1990 to 1999 |
|---|---|
| Deer (crashes with cars) | 300 |
| Bears | 29 |
| Dogs | 18 |
| Snakes | 15 |
| Mountain lions | 6 |
| Sharks | 4 |
| Alligators | 2 |

## WORKSTATION

### The attack on the surfer was a case of mistaken identity.

- Many sharks actually have very good eyesight.
- When a shark sees something that might be food, the shark tests it by taking a bite. If it doesn't like what it tastes, it spits out the mouthful and swims away.

**This great white shark is taste-testing an underwater camera.**

### You explain to the reporter about the way a great white shark attacks its prey.

- The shark swims below the surface, looking up.
- When it sees prey, the shark stalks it from below.
- When the shark attacks prey at the surface, it swims nearly straight up with lightning-fast speed.
- If the prey is small, such as a fish or seal, the shark gulps it down whole.
- If the prey is larger, such as a sea lion, the shark takes a huge bite. It retreats and waits for the prey to bleed to death. Then the shark returns to eat it.

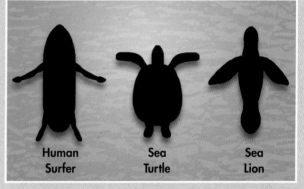

Human Surfer    Sea Turtle    Sea Lion

**You can see by looking at these pictures how a shark could mistake a surfer for another animal.**

### Q CHALLENGE QUESTIONS

1. According to your chart, which animal was responsible for fewer deaths than sharks?
2. Why might a shark mistake a human surfer for a seal?
3. The shark in the picture above didn't eat the camera after all. Why not?

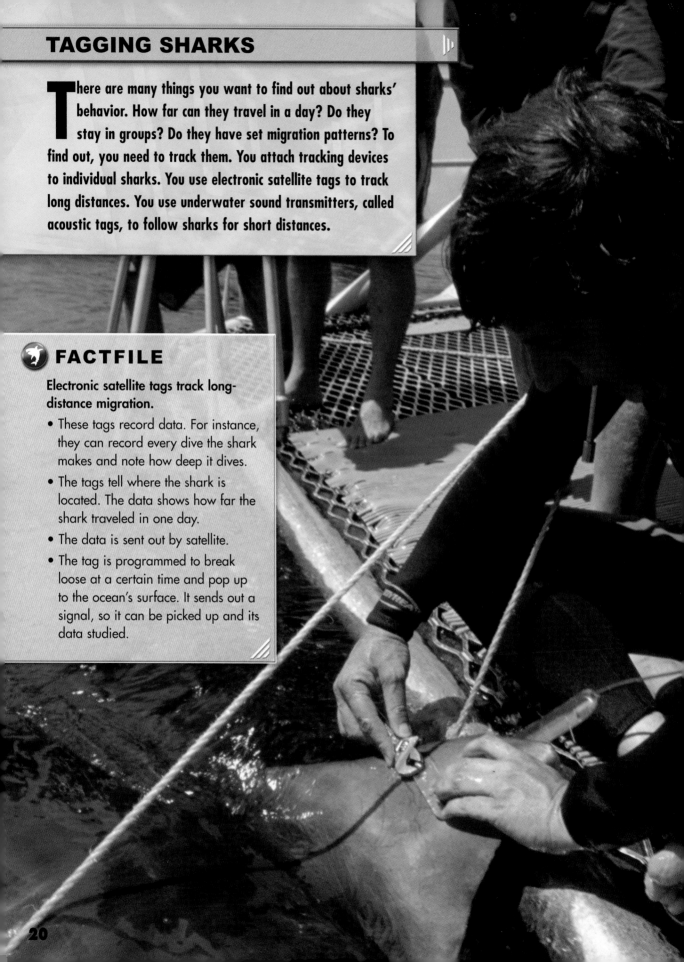

# TAGGING SHARKS

**T**here are many things you want to find out about sharks' behavior. How far can they travel in a day? Do they stay in groups? Do they have set migration patterns? To find out, you need to track them. You attach tracking devices to individual sharks. You use electronic satellite tags to track long distances. You use underwater sound transmitters, called acoustic tags, to follow sharks for short distances.

## FACTFILE

Electronic satellite tags track long-distance migration.

- These tags record data. For instance, they can record every dive the shark makes and note how deep it dives.
- The tags tell where the shark is located. The data shows how far the shark traveled in one day.
- The data is sent out by satellite.
- The tag is programmed to break loose at a certain time and pop up to the ocean's surface. It sends out a signal, so it can be picked up and its data studied.

# WORKSTATION

## Acoustic tags are used to track short-distance travel.

- You attach tags to sharks. The tags give off high-pitched clicks.
- Signal receivers are placed underwater at certain sites.
- Receivers pick up the signals as tagged sharks swim past.
- They show whether a shark is hanging around or revisiting the area.
- They tell how many times the shark was there and when it arrived.

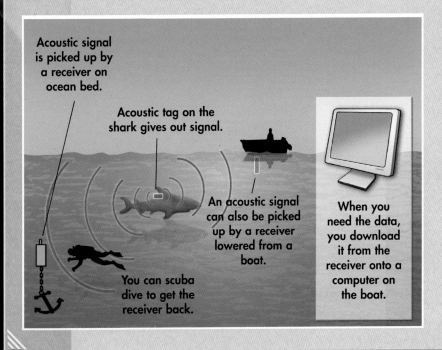

Acoustic signal is picked up by a receiver on ocean bed.

Acoustic tag on the shark gives out signal.

An acoustic signal can also be picked up by a receiver lowered from a boat.

You can scuba dive to get the receiver back.

When you need the data, you download it from the receiver onto a computer on the boat.

## Q CHALLENGE QUESTIONS

Which type of tag would you use for each of these situations?

1. A shark has been visiting two different feeding grounds about 5 miles (8 km) apart. You want to know how often it goes to each place.

2. Every October and November, several sharks show up around an island. You don't see them again until the following year. You want to find out where they have been.

3. You see sharks near the seal colony during the day. You want to know whether they are there at night. It's too dangerous to take a boat out to that area at night.

4. You've tracked two sharks all the way to Hawaii and back. You want to know whether they will return next year, following the same route.

21

# WORKING WITH THE DATA

**B**ack at the lab, you check the location of some of the sharks you tagged a year ago. You've been using acoustic tags to keep track of the feeding grounds they've been visiting. You're looking at two locations in particular. One is a seal colony on a remote stretch of land along the coast. The other is another seal colony on an island about 20 miles (32 km) offshore. You want to know whether the sharks stick to one location or whether they travel back and forth.

## FACTFILE

This map shows the route a great white shark swam in 2004. By tracking the shark, scientists were able to find out for certain that sharks travel from one continent to another. The data about the shark's journey was gathered using an electronic satellite tag. Photographs of the shark's unique fin were taken as further proof.

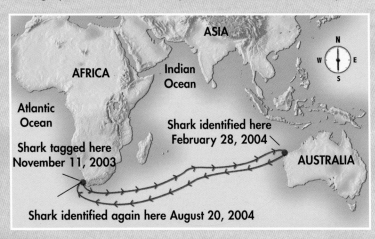

ASIA

AFRICA

Indian Ocean

N
W   E
S

Atlantic Ocean

Shark identified here February 28, 2004

Shark tagged here November 11, 2003

AUSTRALIA

Shark identified again here August 20, 2004

# WORKSTATION

## You track five different sharks at two seal colonies for one year.

Each shark is represented by a different color. A colored dot representing each shark is placed on the graph each week that shark is detected at one of the colonies.

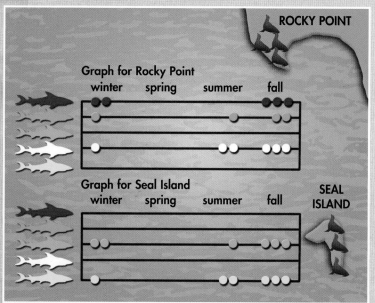

## Looking at the data, you can tell:

- which sharks visit which sites.
- whether one shark tries to keep a site to itself. (That could be an example of territorial behavior.)
- whether any sharks visit both sites.
- whether a shark visits only one site.
- when the sharks visit each site.
- whether the sharks move to certain places in certain seasons.
- whether the sharks' behavior fits a pattern.

## Q CHALLENGE QUESTIONS

1. How many weeks did the blue shark show up at Seal Island during the summer? How about during the winter?
2. In which season did sharks make the most visits to both locations?
3. Are the sharks at either location all year long?
4. Do any sharks move back and forth between the two colonies?

23

You're on an exciting adventure that has taken you to the Sea of Cortez in Mexico. Your mission is to tag hammerhead sharks that gather around a seamount, or submerged mountain. You know that they leave the seamount every evening at sunset. You want to find out how far they travel and where they go. This time, however, you won't be tagging them from a boat. You'll be diving among the hammerheads as you tag them.

## FACTFILE

You've observed some interesting things about hammerheads.

- There can be hundreds of them in a single school.
- They feed on fish, octopus, squid, and crustaceans such as crabs.
- Their cruising speed is about 2 miles (3 km) per hour.

This particular type of hammerhead shark has never been known to attack a human. Still, they're sharks, so you're careful as you dive among them.

- You'll be using both electronic and acoustic tags.
- You'll use electronic satellite tags to track the sharks' long-term movements and diving behavior.
- The acoustic tag data will allow you to follow the shark in a boat overnight, using a portable receiver.

This data shows the routes taken by two sharks tracked overnight. Both began near the top of the seamount and then swam into deeper water. Both would often dive down to the sea bottom. The numbers on this map show the depth of the water.

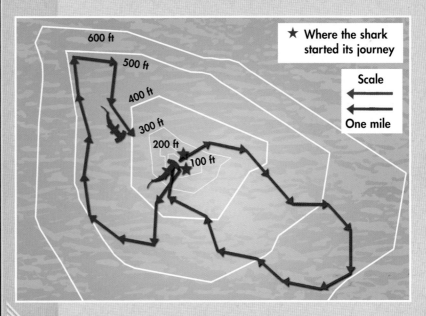

# Q CHALLENGE QUESTIONS

1. How many miles did the red shark travel?
2. How many miles did the blue shark travel?
3. Which shark swam in the deepest water?
4. How many feet down did the blue shark go on its deepest dive to the sea bottom?

# KEEPING A SHARK IN CAPTIVITY

You've hurried back home for an event you wouldn't want to miss. A few weeks ago, a young female great white shark was accidentally caught in a fishing net. You and your team rushed to help rescue her and care for her in an ocean pen. She's been doing well. Now she's ready to be moved to a huge tank at the aquarium. You've been looking forward to this day! You'll be able to study her closely while she lives at the aquarium.

## FACTFILE

The young great white shark will live in this tank for no more than a few months. If she does not do well or gets too big, she will be released back into the ocean. You helped design this tank. When you did so, you had some important things to keep in mind.

- A great white shark would need plenty of room in a rounded tank. Her tank holds more than 1 million gallons (3.8 million liters) of water!
- Sharks are very sensitive to mild electric currents. That might come from electric pumps or, in the ocean, from lightning. Electrical equipment must be placed carefully to make sure that electric currents don't reach the tank.

Many people come to watch the shark. You hope they gain a new respect for sharks, especially great whites.

# WORKSTATION

**The time has come to move the shark from the pen to the aquarium. You and your crew work quickly and carefully.**

- First you net her and lift her onto a stretcher.
- You handle her gently so that you don't scare her.
- You keep her gills wet so she can breathe while she is on the stretcher.
- You transfer her to a specially designed 3,000-gallon (11,356-liter) portable tank on wheels.
- You drive her to the aquarium and release her into her new home!

**You watch the shark as she explores her new surroundings. Your most important job now is making sure that she is eating well.**

This great white shark is one year old. At that age, she should be growing quickly. You keep careful records of how much food she eats. She should be eating 1.5 percent of her body weight every day. While the shark was in the ocean pen, you weighed her every 25 days. You didn't move her to the tank in the aquarium until she was eating well. Here are your notes from the first 200 days:

| Day | 1 | 25 | 50 | 75 | 100 | 125 | 150 | 175 | 200 |
|---|---|---|---|---|---|---|---|---|---|
| Weight of shark (pounds) | 50 | 54 | 63 | 69 | 75 | 81 | 85 | 94 | 100 |
| Pounds of food eaten | 0.50 | 0.83 | 0.95 | 1.17 | 1.20 | 1.30 | 1.87 | 1.41 | 1.50 |
| Percentage of body weight | 0.8% | 1.5% | 1.5% | 1.7% | 1.6% | 1.6% | 2.2% | 1.5% | 1.5% |

## Q CHALLENGE QUESTIONS

1. On which day did the shark begin eating well enough to be moved to the aquarium?
2. On which days had she gained more than 8 pounds?
3. What was the first day that she ate more than 1.5 percent of her body weight?
4. During the period of time between day 125 and day 150, you tried giving her a different type of food. Do you think she liked it? How do you know?

**A**s a shark biologist, you want to help people learn more about sharks. Many people know only that some sharks can be dangerous. They don't know how important these predators are. Other people don't understand that sharks are becoming endangered. About 100 million of them are killed every year for their fins. You do all you can to help people realize why sharks should be protected.

 **FACTFILE**

People often ask what they can do to stay safe when they go swimming. You have some good advice for them.

- Swim with a group of people and stay close to shore.
- Don't swim where there are seals or sea lions.
- Don't wear shiny jewelry in the water. A shark may think it is the glint of a fish's scales.
- Don't swim at night, dawn, or dusk.
- Watch for diving seabirds. They may be after small fish that could also attract sharks.
- Don't try to touch, or otherwise annoy, a shark!

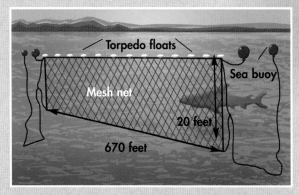

On some beaches, nets like these are used to keep sharks from coming into contact with people. However, other marine life can get tangled up in these nets and die.

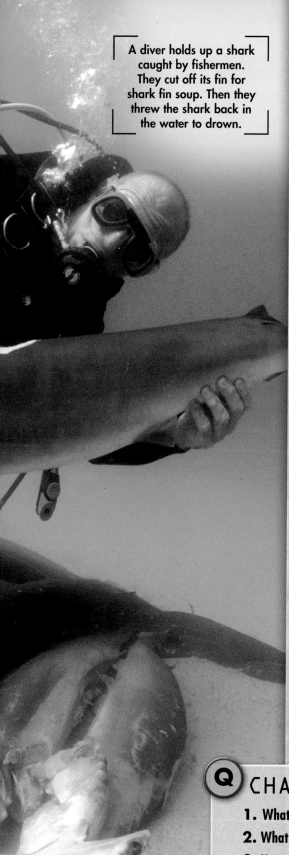

A diver holds up a shark caught by fishermen. They cut off its fin for shark fin soup. Then they threw the shark back in the water to drown.

### Why are sharks important?

- They help control the population of animals that are beneath them on the food chain. This keeps a balance of plant and animal life.
- They take out weak and unhealthy animals. This improves the health of the animals that are left. It also cuts down on competition among those animals for food and space.

### Why have so many sharks been killed?

- Every day, 270,000 sharks are killed worldwide. They are killed out of fear and for sport. They are also killed for body parts to be sold as souvenirs (such as jaws and teeth) or for food.

Shark fin soup is a valued meal in some cultures.

### If the population gets too low, can it recover?

- It is unlikely. People have been catching sharks faster than the sharks can reproduce.
- Some fish, such as tuna, produce thousands of eggs at a time. Female great white sharks, however, give birth to only about 12 pups per breeding season.

## Q CHALLENGE QUESTIONS

1. What is one problem with using shark nets?
2. What are three reasons that so many sharks are killed every day?
3. How do sharks help keep ocean populations in balance?
4. What are two reasons that explain why a shark population cannot recover?

# TIPS FOR SCIENCE SUCCESS

## Pages 6–7
### Shark Biologist

The sharks in these pictures share certain similarities because they belong to one of the 34 shark families. Sharks don't all look alike. They often eat different things, live in different places, and behave in different ways.

## Pages 8–9
### The Design of a Shark

All sharks have shared characteristics, including the way their bodies are put together. If you compared a hammerhead shark with the huge whale shark or the tiny pygmy shark, you'd find they have many things in common. These include skeleton, skin, and arrangement of fins (although some have more fins than others).

## Pages 10–11
### Shark Killers

Experts examine the dead bodies of sharks, just as doctors and crime investigators look inside a human body to find out what caused the person to die. Sometimes the smallest things can bring down a large creature. In this case, many tiny shrimp-like copepods weakened the shark and brought about its death.

## Pages 12–13
### Leaping Sharks!

Many animals show off in one way or another to get the attention of the opposite sex. Also, when animals are hungry, they will make an extra effort to catch food that is good for their body. A seal's high percentage of blubber will provide a shark with the most energy.

## Pages 14–15
### Top Predators

Every living thing is part of a food chain. In fact, most are usually part of a few different food chains. These join up to make a food web. Most animals are in the middle of the chain, trying to eat while not becoming another animal's dinner. Like sharks, we are at the top of our food chain.

## Pages 16–17
### Staying Warm in Cold Water

Sharks are one of the few types of fish that are warm-bodied rather than cold-blooded. When it's cold outside, cold-blooded animals, such as reptiles and most fish, have to warm up before they can move very well. That's why you often see a snake or lizard sunning itself on a rock.

## Pages 20–21
### Tagging Sharks

Satellite tagging has made it possible to find out things about animal behavior that we couldn't have learned otherwise. In the past, sharks were tagged with a simple plastic tag. Scientists couldn't find out where that shark went unless it was killed and someone sent the scientists the tag. The scientists could tell only where the shark was when it was tagged and where it died. Now we can follow the movements of sharks as they go about their lives.

## Pages 26–27
### Keeping a Shark in Captivity

Some types of sharks adapt well to living in an aquarium. Many attempts have been made to keep a great white shark in captivity. For years, few sharks survived in tanks for more than a few days. Then, in 2003, a young female great white shark was kept in a 1 million-gallon (3.8 million-liter) tank at Monterey Bay Aquarium in California. She was released after 198 days.

## Pages 28–29
### Looking to the Future

There are many different careers in the field of marine biology. Someone who wants to be a marine biologist or scientist should take lots of math and science classes in school. It's also good to learn as much as possible about computers and technology.